GW01158686

MUSICAL INSTRUMENTS

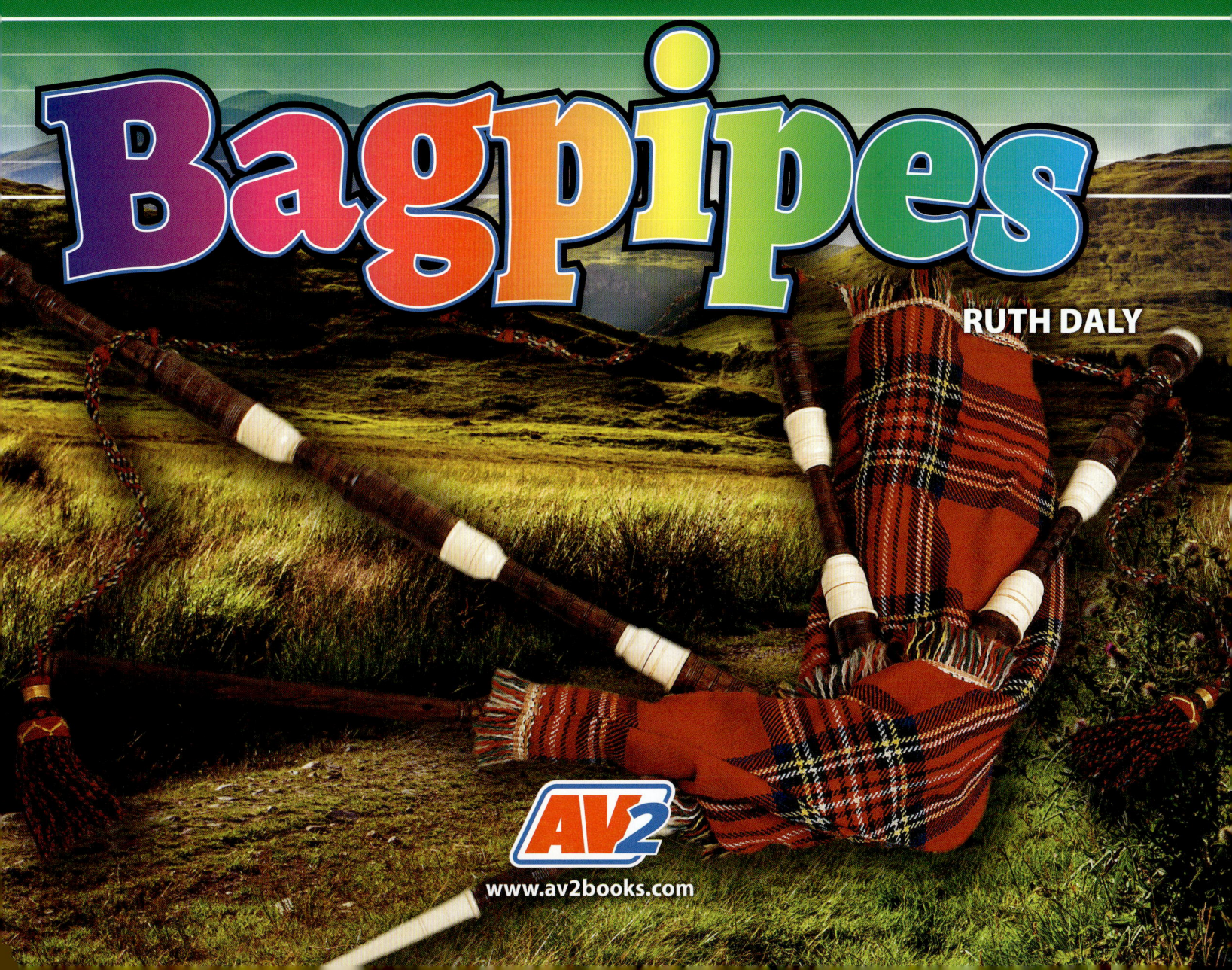

Bagpipes

RUTH DALY

AV2
www.av2books.com

AV2

Step 1
Go to www.av2books.com

Step 2
Enter this unique code
JVLZTEFPV

Step 3
Explore your interactive eBook!

Bagpipes
MUSICAL INSTRUMENTS

Start!

AV2 is optimized for use on any device

Your interactive eBook comes with...

Read

Audio
Listen to the entire book read aloud

Videos
Watch informative video clips

Weblinks
Gain additional information for research

Try This!
Complete activities and hands-on experiments

Key Words
Study vocabulary, and complete a matching word activity

Quizzes
Test your knowledge

Slideshows
View images and captions

View new titles and product videos at www.av2books.com

2

MUSICAL INSTRUMENTS

Bagpipes Contents

- 2   AV2 Book Code
- 4   Time to Play the Bagpipes
- 6   Bagpipe Parts
- 8   Playing the Bagpipes
- 10   Pipes
- 12   Drones
- 14   Bagpipe Materials
- 16   Bagpipe History
- 18   Types of Music
- 20   Playing Together
- 22   Know Your Instruments
- 24   Key Words

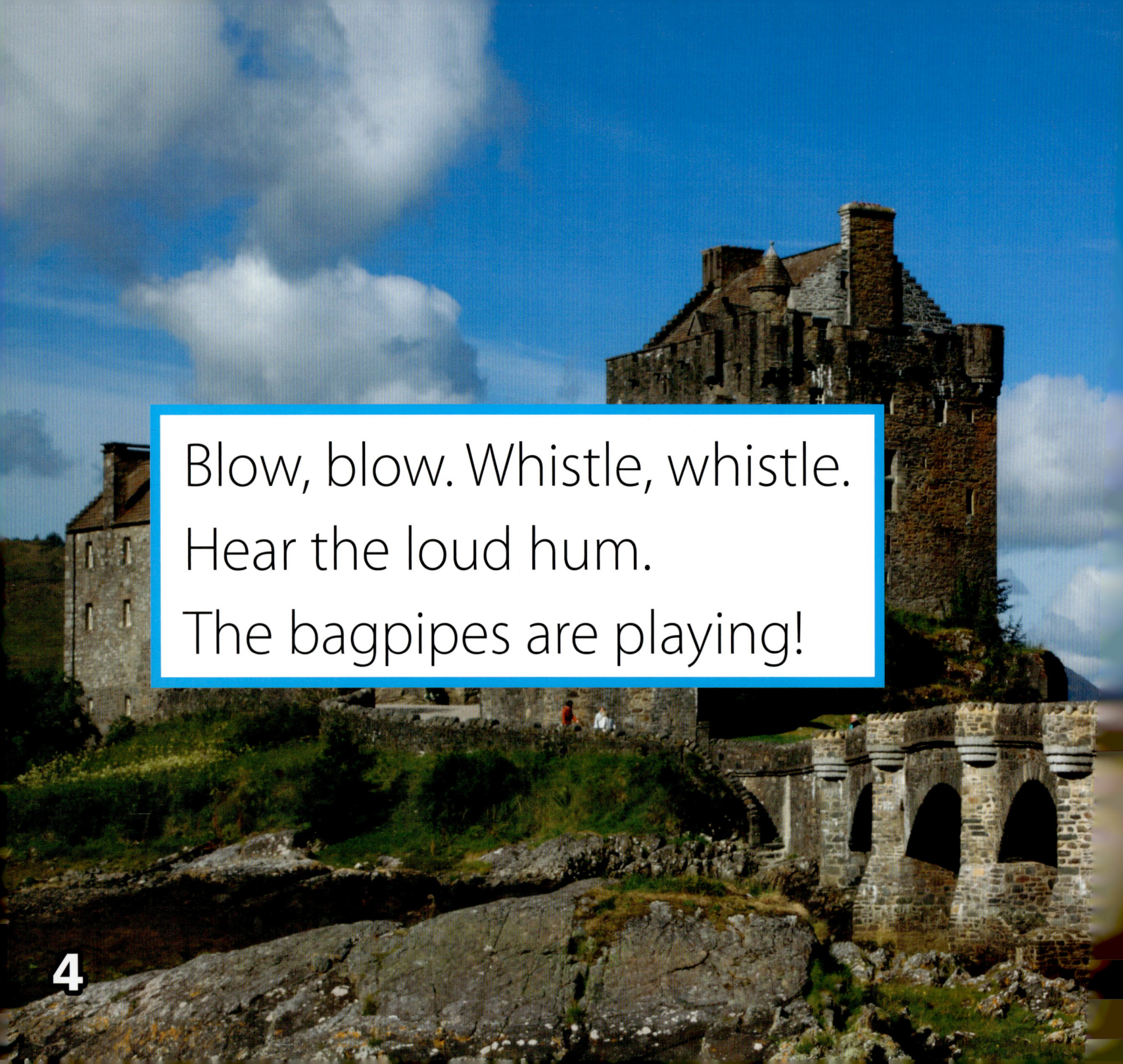

Blow, blow. Whistle, whistle.
Hear the loud hum.
The bagpipes are playing!

5

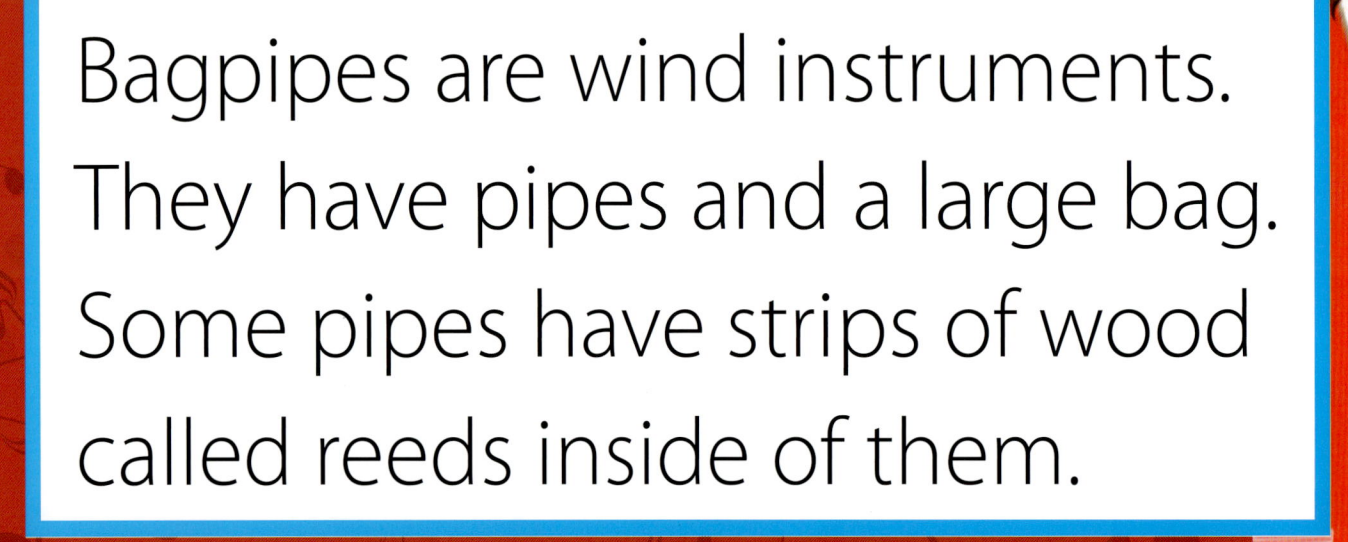

Bagpipes are wind instruments. They have pipes and a large bag. Some pipes have strips of wood called reeds inside of them.

Most bagpipes have five pipes. One is called the blowpipe.

7

8

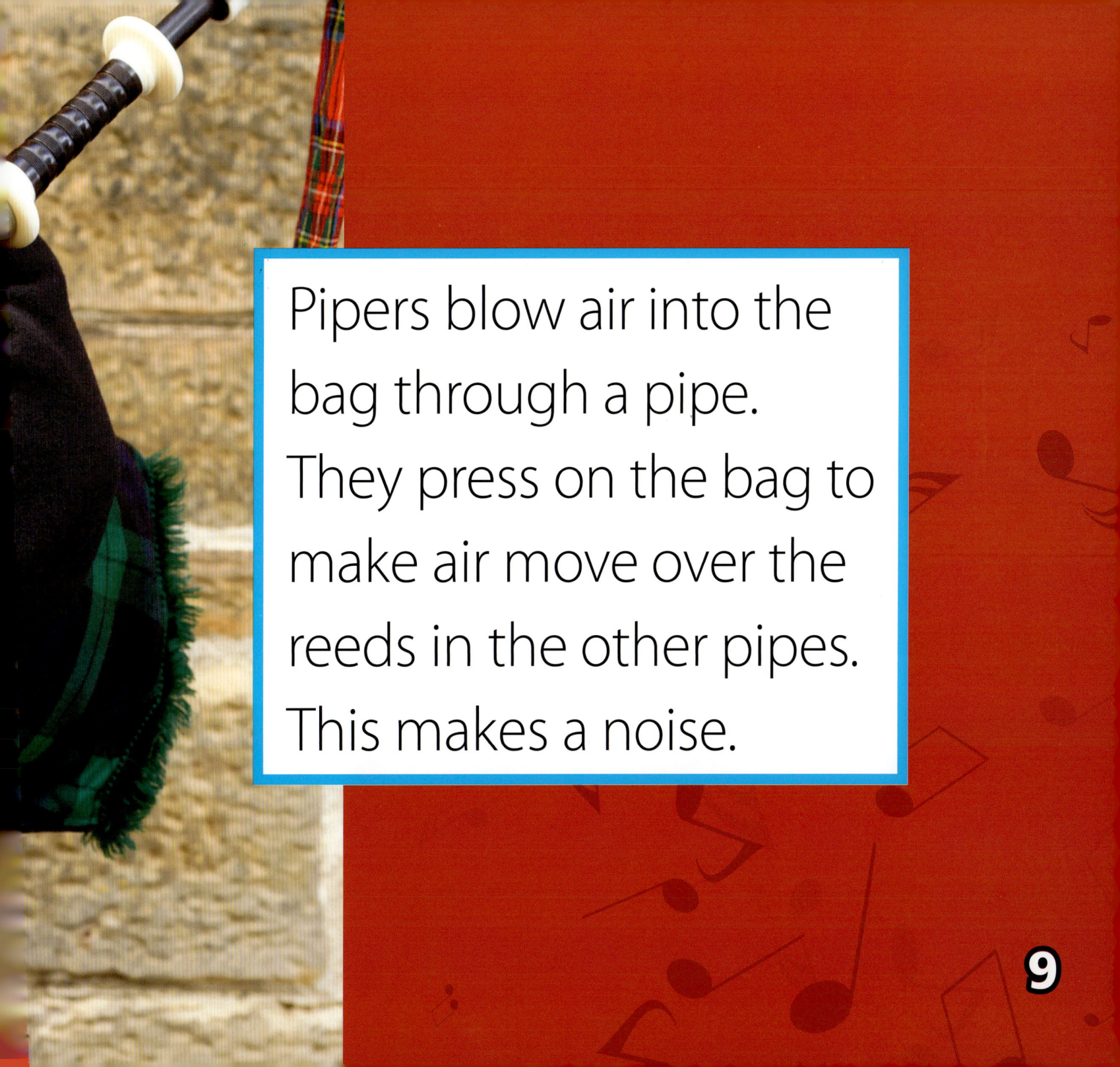

Pipers blow air into the bag through a pipe. They press on the bag to make air move over the reeds in the other pipes. This makes a noise.

One pipe has finger holes. Pipers cover the holes with their fingers. This changes the sound.

11

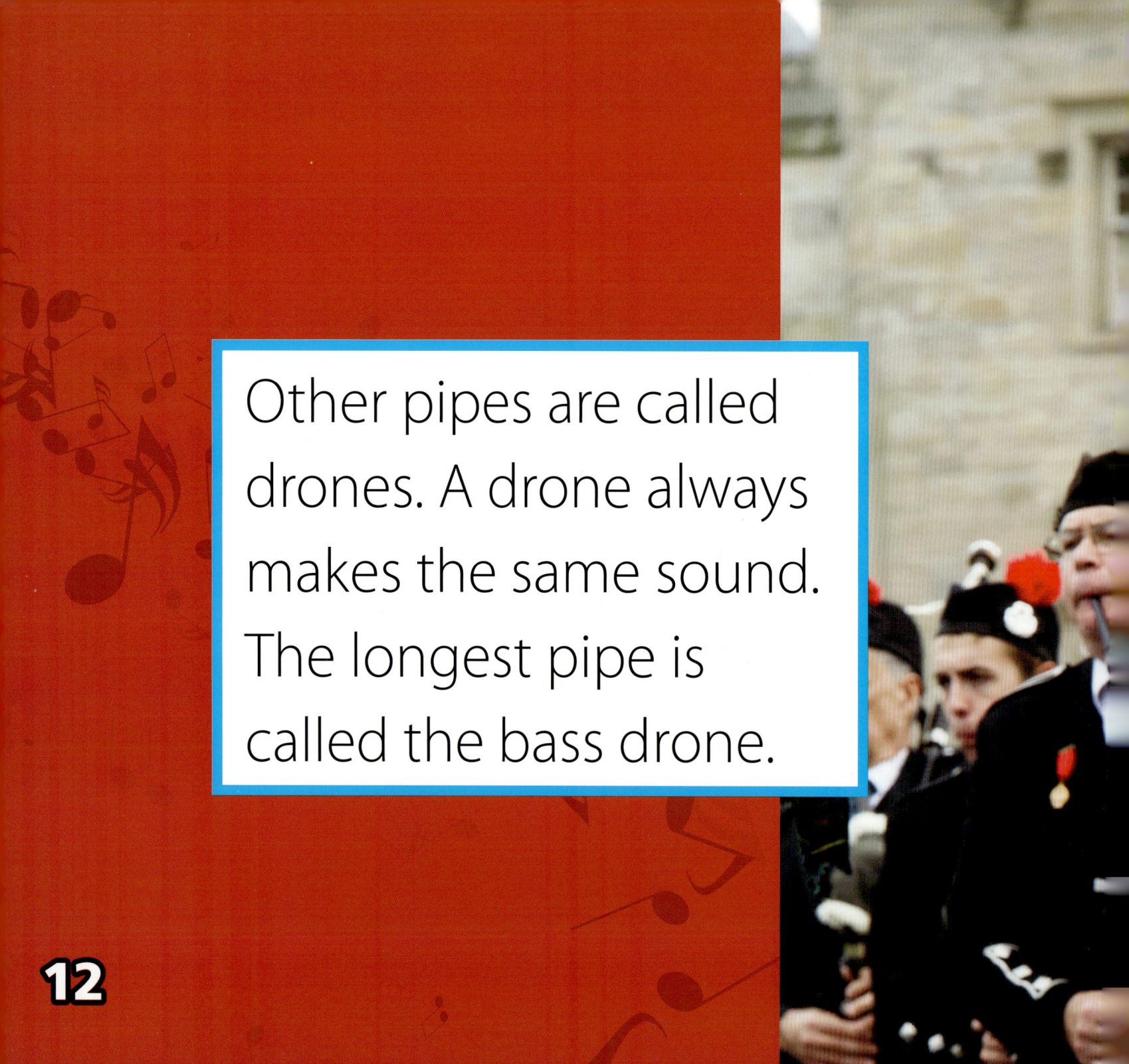

Other pipes are called drones. A drone always makes the same sound. The longest pipe is called the bass drone.

13

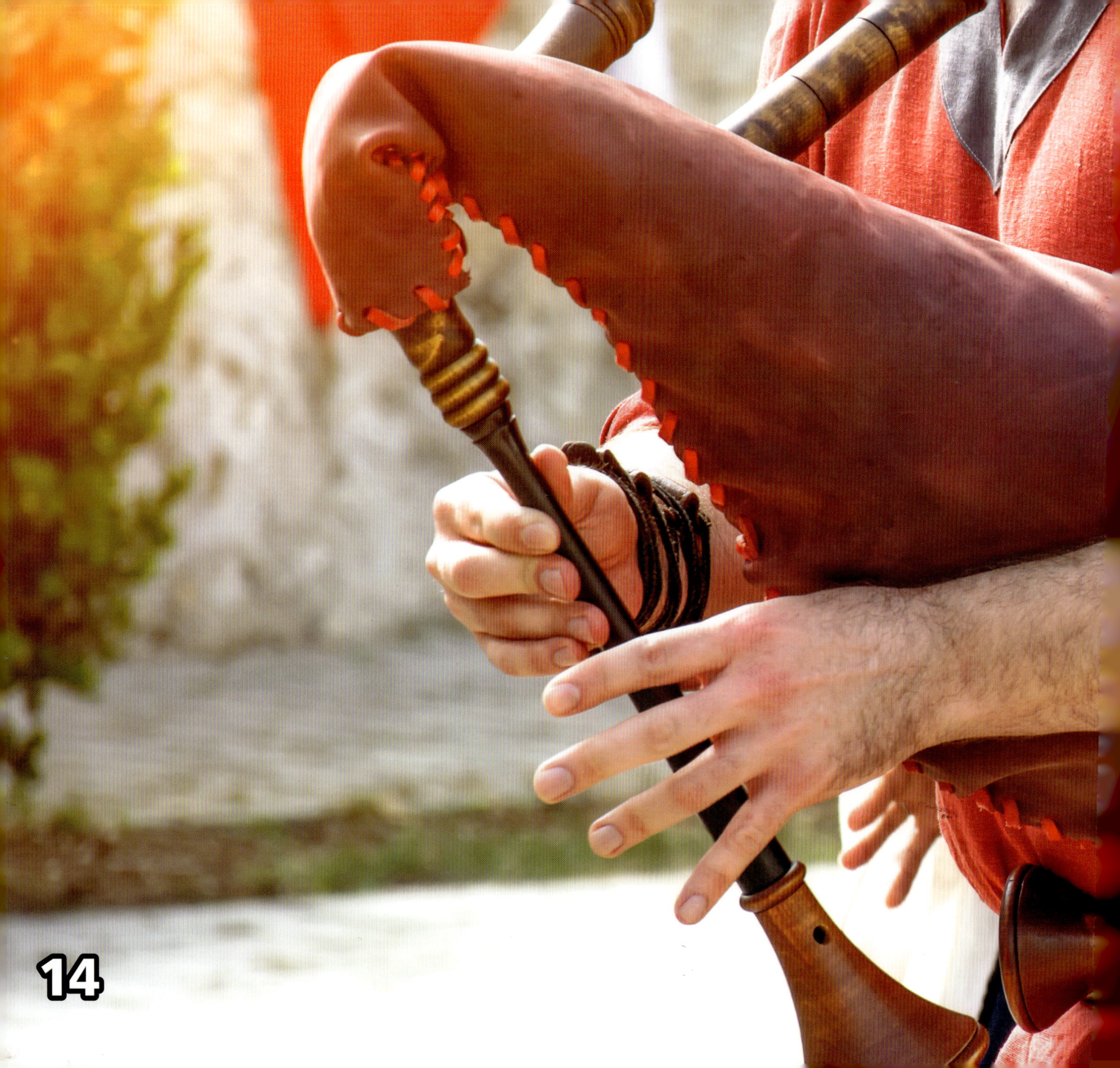

The bagpipe's bag is made from leather or rubber.
It is covered in fabric.
The pipes are plastic or wood.

Bagpipes have been played in Scotland for many years. They were once used in wars. Their sound scared the enemy.

Bagpipes were invented in Egypt more than 2,000 years ago.

17

18

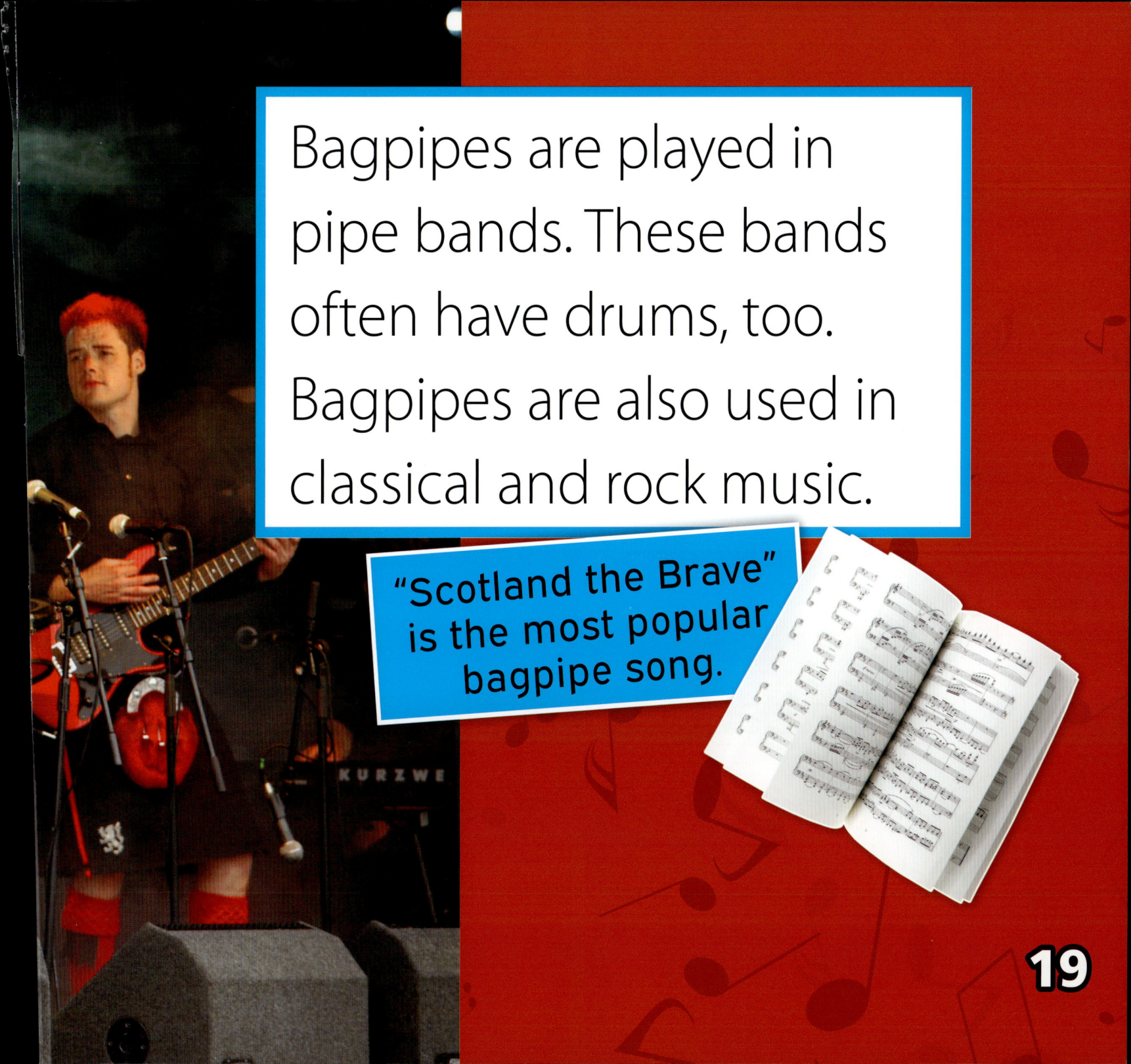

Bagpipes are played in pipe bands. These bands often have drums, too. Bagpipes are also used in classical and rock music.

"Scotland the Brave" is the most popular bagpipe song.

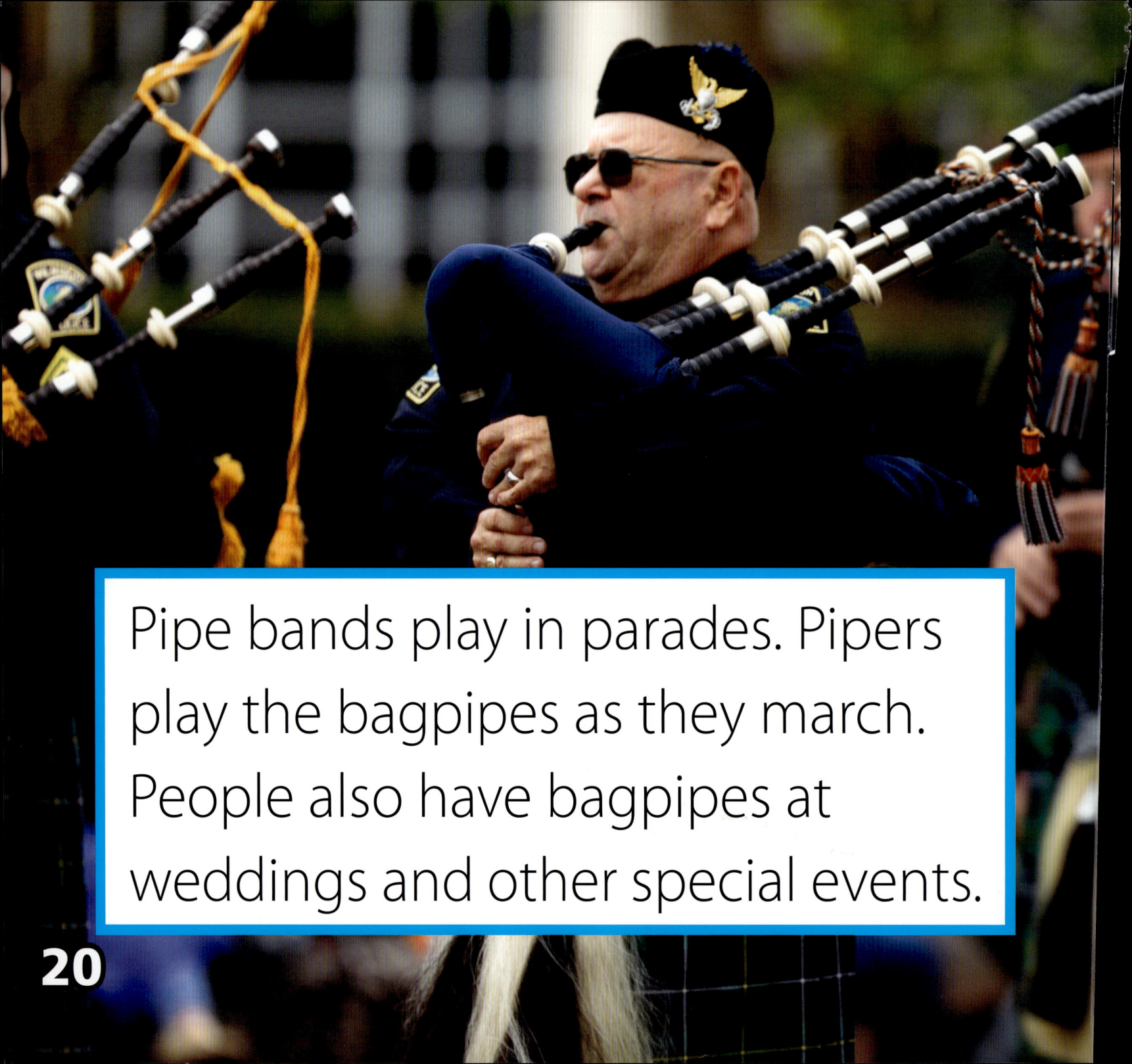

Pipe bands play in parades. Pipers play the bagpipes as they march. People also have bagpipes at weddings and other special events.

21

See what you have learned about bagpipes.

22

Which of these pictures does not show bagpipes?

23

KEY WORDS

Research has shown that as much as 65 percent of all written material published in English is made up of 300 words. These 300 words cannot be taught using pictures or learned by sounding them out. They must be recognized by sight. This book contains 54 common sight words to help young readers improve their reading fluency and comprehension. This book also teaches young readers several important content words, such as proper nouns. These words are paired with pictures to aid in learning and improve understanding.

Page	Sight Words First Appearance
4	are, hear, the
6	a, and, have, is, large, most, of, one, some, them, they
9	air, in, into, make, move, on, other, over, this, through, to
10	changes, has, sound, their, with
12	always, same
15	from, it, made, or
16	been, for, many, more, once, than, used, were, years
19	also, often, song, these, too
20	as, at, people, play

Page	Content Words First Appearance
4	bagpipes, hum
6	bag, blowpipe, pipes, reeds, strips, wind instruments, wood
9	noise, pipers
10	fingers, holes
12	drones
15	fabric, leather, plastic, rubber
16	Egypt, enemy, Scotland, wars
19	classical music, drums, pipe bands, rock music, "Scotland the Brave"
20	events, parades, weddings

Published by AV2
350 5th Avenue, 59th Floor New York, NY 10118
Website: www.av2books.com

Copyright ©2021 AV2
All rights reserved. No part of this publication may be reproduced, stored in a retrieval system, or transmitted in any form or by any means, electronic, mechanical, photocopying, recording, or otherwise, without the prior written permission of the publisher.

Library of Congress Cataloging-in-Publication Data

Names: Daly, Ruth, 1962- author.
Title: Bagpipes / Ruth Daly.
Description: New York : AV2, 2020. | Series: Musical instruments |
Audience: Ages 6-9 | Audience: Grades K-1 |
Identifiers: LCCN 2019042788 (print) | LCCN 2019042789 (ebook) | ISBN 9781791116323 (library binding) |
ISBN 9781791116330 (paperback) | ISBN 9781791116347 | ISBN 9781791116354
Subjects: LCSH: Bagpipe--Juvenile literature.

Classification: LCC ML980 D35 2020 (print) | LCC ML980 (ebook) | DDC 788.4/919--dc23
LC record available at https://lccn.loc.gov/2019042788
LC ebook record available at https://lccn.loc.gov/2019042789

Printed in Guangzhou, China
1 2 3 4 5 6 7 8 9 0 24 23 22 21 20

022020
100919

Project Coordinator: John Willis   Designer: Ana María Vidal

The publisher acknowledges Alamy, Dreamstime, Getty Images, iStock, and Shutterstock as the primary image suppliers for this title.